The SPORTS HEROES Library

Hockey's
SUPER
SCORERS

Nathan Aaseng

 Lerner Publications Company • Minneapolis

ACKNOWLEDGMENTS: The photographs are reproduced through the courtesy of: pp. 4, 6, 18, 24, 41, Al Ruelle; pp. 8, 15, 16, 42, 51, 66, United Press International, Inc.; pp. 11, 12, 44, 47, New York Islanders; pp. 21 (David Bier), 26 (Willie Dagenais), Montreal Canadiens; p. 29, Detroit Red Wings; pp. 30, 32, 33, Los Angeles Kings; pp. 37 (Andrew Pichette), 39, Quebec Nordiques; pp. 49, 70, 74, 75, 77, 78, Bruce Bennett; pp. 55, 56, 59, 60, Robert B. Shaver; p. 63, Minnesota North Stars; pp. 64, 65, 68, Bruce Bisping. Cover photograph by Bruce Bennett.

LIBRARY OF CONGRESS CATALOGING IN PUBLICATION DATA

Aaseng, Nathan.
 Hockey's super scorers.

 (The Sports heroes library)
 Summary: Profiles of eight hockey stars known for their high scoring: Mike Bossy, Guy Lafleur, Marcel Dionne, Peter Stastny, Bryan Trottier, Gilbert Perreault, Dino Ciccarelli, and Wayne Gretzky.
 1. Hockey players — Biography — Juvenile literature.
 2. National Hockey League — Juvenile literature.
 [1. Hockey players] I. Title. II. Series.
 GV848.5.A1A25 1984   796.96′2′0922 [B] [920] 83-17511
 ISBN 0-8225-1340-4

Manufactured in the United States of America

International Standard Book Number: 0-8225-1340-4
Library of Congress Catalog Card Number: 83-17511

1 2 3 4 5 6 7 8 9 10 93 92 91 90 89 88 87 86 85 84

Contents

Introduction   5

1 Mike Bossy   9

2 Guy Lafleur   19

3 Marcel Dionne   27

4 Peter Stastny   35

5 Bryan Trottier   45

6 Gilbert Perreault   53

7 Dino Ciccarelli   61

8 Wayne Gretzky   71

Practice helps Peter Stastny master such skills as winning face-offs. But it takes more than just practice to be a top goal-scorer. What's his secret?

Introduction

What is the secret to getting that little rubber puck into the net? Many hockey players have worked themselves into exhaustion trying to find out. Most have been skating since the age of three, so by the time they have reached the National Hockey League, they usually have had a dozen years of experience in organized leagues. Countless hours have been spent learning how to control the puck with a stick, how to pass, how to receive a pass, and how to shoot wrist shots, slap shots, and backhands. They've sweated through hundreds of practices learning how to check, how to battle in the corners, how to win face-offs, how to keep their position on the ice. Will all of this make them expert goal scorers?

Not likely. All the instruction in the world may turn out good all-around hockey players, but it won't teach much about the most crucial hockey skill of all: how to get a puck past a goalie.

Goal scoring is not a science; it is a special art. It is something that hockey's top offensive stars

Ace goal scorer Mike Bossy shoots past Boston Bruin goalie Pete Peeters without even looking at the puck.

do naturally without thinking. Most say there is really no way to practice scoring technique. Unless you are born with the instinct or stumble across ways to score, you're out of luck.

This book takes a look at eight NHL stars who own the talent of lighting up the red lights behind the net. Their skills are so mysterious that even they don't know the secrets that have made them successful. As you might expect, there is no pattern

6

that all eight follow in collecting their scores. Guy Lafleur seems to be out to break the sound barrier as he zooms down the ice and unloads a blistering slap shot. Mike Bossy flits in and out of the action, stopping just long enough to flip a loose puck into the cage. Wayne Gretzky practices a chess game in motion as he glides along the ice, one step ahead of his opponents.

These artists have helped turn the game of professional hockey from an all-star wrestling exhibition back into a game of speed and skill. Throughout the 1970s, many hockey promoters believed that brawls and intimidation were the only ways to win games and draw fans. But these players have proven that to be nonsense. Far and away the most popular and skilled players in the game, they rarely see the inside of a penalty box. Most of them are outspoken in their efforts to eliminate dirty play.

But the best arguments of these players are actions, not words. The flurry of action that they bring to the game has made them the center of attention in hockey. When a Wayne Gretzky or a Dino Ciccarelli leads a charge, you can almost feel the tension in the air, and you can certainly hear it from the noise of the fans. These eight magical marksmen, hockey's super scorers, have become the hottest things on ice.

One of hockey's familiar sights is Bossy giving the traditional arms-up signal that a goal has been made. This was Bossy's third of the game in 1983 play-off action against Boston.

1
Mike
Bossy

Mike Bossy owns one of the most feared shots in hockey. But it's not because goalies are afraid of being hit by it. What worries them is that there's a good chance they *won't* be hit! Bossy's relatively soft shots may be easy on a goalie's body, but they're awfully rough on his mind. After awhile, it gets discouraging to block most of the net only to see Mike swat the puck into the one unprotected spot. The fact that Mike rarely aims his shot and often doesn't even look at the goal while shooting makes him a frustrating puzzle.

Mike was born in Montreal, Quebec, in 1957, the sixth of ten children. His parents gave him an early feel for the national sport by giving him a toy hockey stick when he was just a few days old. From there he followed the route of many Canadian hockey stars: a pair of skates at the age of three, a backyard rink, and an early entry into an organized league.

Fortunately for Mike, he didn't have to leave home as a young teenager to join a junior league team, as did many boys. Instead he could stay at home and play for the Laval Nationals in the Quebec Junior Hockey League. Bossy quickly found that he had a touch for scoring goals, and he scored 308 during his four years as a junior. Expecting to be snatched quickly in the 1977 NHL draft, Mike was stunned when the first 14 teams ignored him. It was the price he had to pay for taking it easy in the junior leagues. Scouts complained that all he could do was shoot. They questioned whether a kid who didn't check and couldn't play defense would make it as a pro.

The New York Islanders, however, were looking for a scorer, and Bossy seemed the perfect answer. They selected him with their first-round pick and immediately placed him on a forward line with star center Bryan Trottier and powerful left winger Clark Gillies.

The sudden plunge into the NHL was almost too much for Mike. He had never lived away from home before and didn't look forward to a season in a New York hotel. He had problems fitting in with the team and was so shy that, at first, he didn't tell the team his name was Michael and not the

Mike Bossy

French Michel that was printed in the press guide.

Trottier helped solve the problem by inviting Mike and his wife to stay at his house. That was the beginning of both a good friendship and one of the most awesome scoring combinations in the pros. Trottier and Bossy worked so well together that, along with Gillies, they became known as the Trio Grande. That season Bossy scored 53 goals, which easily broke Richard Martin's rookie goal record of 44. His sharpshooting especially paid off on power plays. He scored 25 of his goals with the opposition shorthanded.

Alone and unnoticed near the boards, Bossy prepares to dart into the action to snap a loose puck into the goal.

Despite this brilliant start, there was talk that Mike wasn't tough enough to be a pro star. Even his own coach seemed to agree. During the 1978 Stanley Cup series with Toronto, Mike was often benched in favor of the more rugged Bob Nystrom. When Bossy did see action in game six, he was blasted against the boards in a corner and had to be carried off the ice.

During the 1978-79 season, Mike made up his mind to prove his critics wrong. Although he refused to be drawn into fights, he knew there were other ways to prove his worth. He learned how to go into the dangerous corners without getting smashed, and he started to throw his 185 pounds around on checks. While Bossy kept his attention on defense, the rest of the league was talking about his scoring. His 69 goals led the NHL and, with 151 goals, Bossy-Trottier-Gillies broke the previous mark for goals scored by a line.

The baffling question was, How did he do it? Bossy couldn't shoot as hard as many pros. Others could shoot more accurately. (In fact, Mike once missed an open net from center ice twice in the same period!) Hockey reporters went digging to find the key to his success. They came up with three.

Bossy's greatest talent seemed to be his quick wrists. He could get his shots off so quickly that goalies had no time to prepare. His favorite shot was the wrist shot, which he managed by snapping the blade of his stick off the ice.

Experts also mentioned Mike's knack of skating without the puck. Most of Bossy's goals came from shots 10 to 15 feet in front of the goal. Mike darted in and out of that area, seeming to disappear and then suddenly reappear in front of the goal. Like a basketball player cutting towards the basket, Bossy kept working to get himself open in case a pass ever came. If a rebound or a pass slid in front of the net, Mike would scoot in to shoot the puck before others could locate it.

Bossy's third talent just couldn't be explained logically. The pros claimed he had a "sixth sense." Somehow, he instinctively knew where to shoot the puck. Mike found the tiniest openings without looking, which convinced him that it was a waste of time to practice his shots.

The Bossy style showed up in a key goal in the Islanders' 1980 Stanley Cup final against the Philadelphia Flyers. New York led, three games to two, and then battled the Flyers in a close sixth game. With the score tied at 2-2 in the second period, the Islanders fired a shot at the Flyer net. The puck slid out in front of the goal. Before anyone else could react, Bossy gave it a little flick, and the Islanders led, 3-2. Mike totaled 10 goals and 13 assists as New York swept to its first title.

In 1980-81, Bossy set his sights on Rocket Richard's long-standing record of 50 goals in 50 games. After 47 games, the Islander star had 48 goals and seemed a good bet to tie or beat the mark. But opponents clamped down on him, and

It wasn't easy, but Mike managed to tie Rocket Richard's record of 50 goals in 50 games.

he was held scoreless in the next two games. Needing two goals in game number 50, Bossy went through two terrible periods without getting so much as a decent shot on goal. With five minutes to go in the contest, he still hadn't scored. Suddenly, Mike's net-seeking missiles found their mark. Bossy scored two goals to beat the Quebec Nordiques and tie Richard's famous mark.

The Islanders' deadly scoring duo of Bossy (22) and Bryan Trottier (19) celebrate Mike's goal against the Minnesota North Stars in the 1981 Stanley Cup finals.

That season Mike drilled 68 goals in all as the Islanders proved they were the best team in the league. With Bossy scoring a play-off record of 35 points on 17 goals and 18 assists, the Islanders easily defended their title.

Had Wayne Gretzky not come along, 1981-82 would have earned Mike headlines throughout the continent. His total of 64 goals and 83 assists for

147 points was the fourth best offensive showing in NHL history. Unfortunately for Mike, Gretzky put all scoring records to shame that year, and Bossy had to content himself with winning a third straight Stanley Cup.

Bossy kept up his hot pace the next season with 60 more goals. That made him the first NHL player ever to score 50 or more goals in each of his first six seasons. And after a slow start in the play-offs, he again came through with needed goals for his team. Despite being watched closely by the Boston Bruins, Mike scored the game-winning goal in all four Islander wins in that series! In the final game of their match against the highly rated Bruins and their All-Star goalie Pete Peeters, Bossy slammed in four goals to wrap up the series. Mike finished the play-offs with a team-leading 17 goals as New York breezed to their fourth straight Stanley Cup.

Perhaps the secret to Mike Bossy's amazing success was best expressed many years ago by baseball star Willie Keeler. "I hit 'em where they ain't," said Keeler. That ability has made Bossy the best pure shooter in the NHL.

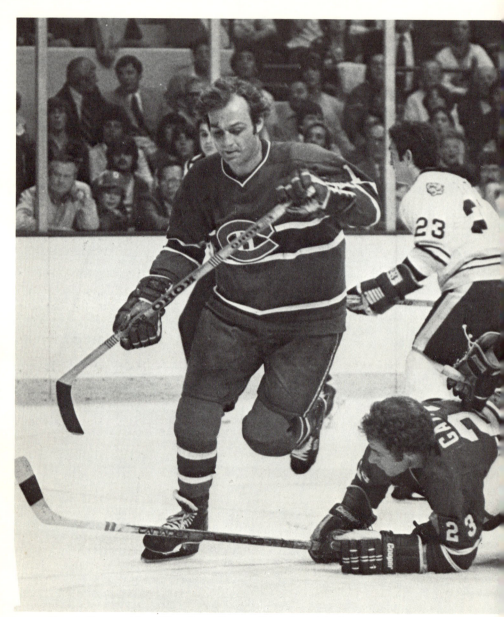

Guy Lafleur, pride of the Canadiens, glides through the mayhem in the 1979 play-offs against Boston.

18

2
Guy
Lafleur

Hockey is more than just a game in Montreal, Quebec. The pride and tradition of the Flying French Canadiens run so deep that the city takes it very seriously. Fans there once started a riot when star player Rocket Richard was suspended in Stanley Cup play. Most of the time, the Canadiens have lived up to their fans' high expectations. In the past 30 years, they have won more Stanley Cup championships than all other teams combined! No other team can boast of such a long line of hockey stars: Doug Harvey, Richard, Jean Beliveau, and Jacques Plante. None of these players, however, have thrilled fans at the Montreal Forum more than Guy Lafleur.

Guy was born in the small river town of Thurso, Ontario, in 1951. Dreams of being a hockey star came early to him. His parents once found him sleeping in a new hockey uniform they had bought for him. His group of friends owned one Canadien jersey among them, and Guy would fight for the right to wear it when they played. Later, he always wore Jean Beliveau's number 4 and kept a poster of the Montreal star.

When Guy was eight, his coach cut a hole in the boards around the rink to provide a target for him. Guy shot at the holes and developed a variety of hard, accurate shots. By the age of 17, Lafleur had advanced far beyond the level of his rivals while playing for the Quebec Junior Aces of the Quebec Junior Hockey League.

The Montreal scouts were convinced that this youngster was the player who could keep the championships coming their way. Although Lafleur was still three years away from draft age in 1968, the Canadiens began scheming to get him. Their first move was to trade for the California Seals' top 1971 draft choice. As they had hoped, when 1971 came around, the hapless Seals were still in bad shape. If the Seals finished last in the standings, they would be giving Montreal the first choice in the entire draft. When the Los Angeles Kings threatened to finish with a worse record than the Seals, the Canadiens rushed in emergency relief and traded the capable Ralph Backstrom to the Kings.

Guy Lafleur

The strategy worked! California fell into last place, and Montreal took over their first choice. Since Lafleur had scored 130 goals in his final year in the junior leagues, Montreal was more certain than ever that he was their man.

When Jean Beliveau retired before the 1971-72 season, Lafleur was expected to take his place at once. He was switched from his right wing position to center, but he never got comfortable there. Moved back to right wing, he scored 29 and 28 goals in his first seasons. Those were fine totals for a young player, but hardly what the Canadien fans expected from this latest superstar. As the criticism grew, Guy hid from the press and spent a lot of time alone writing depressing poetry. Montreal was so afraid the homesick Lafleur would move back to Quebec of the new World Hockey League that they offered him a new, rich contract before the 1973-74 season. That must have seemed a waste to many when Guy slipped to just 21 goals and scored none in the play-offs.

During the summer, Lafleur was jolted by a public scolding from his old idol, Beliveau. Taking the star's advice to get to work, Guy charged into training camp with a new attitude. Throwing away his helmet, he began to take chances and to play aggressively. For the first time, Lafleur showed the Canadiens the furious, nonstop assault on goal that he had displayed as a youth. Even though he lost ice time due to a broken finger, Guy scored 53 goals and assisted on 66. He added 12 more goals in Montreal's unsuccessful bid for the Stanley Cup.

With Lafleur supplying the firepower, the Canadiens began to regain their old magic. In 1975-76, Lafleur captured the first of three straight scoring titles with 56 goals and 69 assists. Montreal's game of speed and sharp passing, meanwhile, ended the bruising Philadelphia Flyers' reign as NHL champs.

That season was a sneak preview of the Canadiens' awesome 1976-77 season. Montreal stormed through the schedule with a 60-8-12 mark for 132 points, more than any team in NHL history. Lafleur again led the way with a league-leading 136 points on 56 goals and 80 assists. Continuing to tear up the opposition in the play-offs, the Canadien star added 9 goals and 17 assists. He easily won the Conn Smythe Trophy as the Most Valuable Player in the play-offs, as Montreal pounded Boston to win the finals in four straight games.

Guy's success could be traced to the fact that he simply had about as much talent as could be packed into a single human being. His teammates would show up at training camp, thinking their summer of workouts had put them in good shape. Lafleur would then come in, lace up his skates for the first time since last season, and proceed to zoom past everyone from the start of practice to the end! With his easy, smooth stride, Lafleur seemed to be only cruising around the ice while others strained and puffed to keep up.

Guy also happened to be built perfectly for both speed and power. At 6 feet and 175 pounds, he could race in at blinding speed and then wind up for a powerful slap shot. The combined speeds of his body and his stick sent the puck rocketing toward the net. Experts in a 1980 *Sport* magazine poll rated his shot as the toughest to stop in the game.

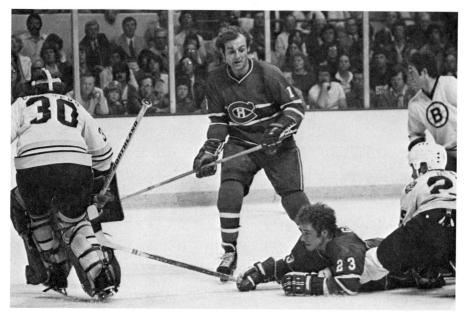

Lafleur had to pick up his struggling teammates with clutch plays in the 1979 Stanley Cup play-offs.

One thing Lafleur did not have were nerves of steel. Guy had such problems staying calm that he was known to suit up for games more than five hours ahead of time. Sometimes he just sat, waiting nervously, and at other times he whacked the floor with hockey sticks to help burn off energy. Surprisingly, the high-strung star held up well to the tremendous demands of the Montreal fans. During his prime, Montreal papers printed practically his every word and sneeze.

Some of Lafleur's top play-off moments have come against the Boston Bruins. Perhaps the most memorable was the 1979 semifinal. The Bruins, threatening to end Montreal's string of championships, tied the series at three games each and took a 3-1 lead in the final game. Boston goalie Gilles Gilbert played especially well, stopping 27 shots in the first two periods. But with six minutes left, Lafleur fed Mark Napier for a score. Two minutes later, he worked the puck to Guy Lapointe for the tying goal. Each team scored once more, sending the game into overtime. Just one minute into the extra period, Lafleur sped down the ice. In full flight, he wound up with a slap shot from just inside the blue line. The puck hit the back of the net before the goalie could move, and Montreal claimed another win.

Iron-man Lafleur rarely missed a game and became the first NHL player to score 50 or more goals in six straight years. But nagging injuries held him out of almost 30 contests in 1980-81, and his scoring fell off. It seemed that he never quite recovered from the collision of the previous spring when he had fallen asleep while driving. The injured star scored only 27 goals in 1980-81, and none in the play-offs. Although he continued to rank among the Canadiens' top scorers in the next several seasons, he no longer challenged for the NHL scoring title.

Immediately, Wayne Gretzky took over as the

Guy winds up for a slap shot against the Los Angeles Kings.

game's top offensive star. But no one could take the place of Lafleur in history or in the hearts of the Canadien fans. With his graceful, racehorse style of play, he was the best example of the kind of play that has made the Montreal Canadiens the most successful and the most exciting team in NHL history. Pro coaches agreed that, during Montreal's stranglehold on the Stanley Cup in the 1970s, Guy Lafleur was the one player in hockey who could win a game by himself.

3
Marcel
Dionne

Marcel Dionne has spent most of his pro career playing hockey in Southern California. That makes about as much sense as sending a top pearl diver to work in the Arctic! As a result, one of hockey's best skaters and most brilliant offensive artists has played before sparse crowds in a city where the only ice most people see comes out of a freezer. Marcel was the superstar who was supposed to turn sunny Los Angeles into a hotbed of hockey madness. Not even Dionne has managed that, but he has given the Los Angeles Kings their money's worth in offensive fireworks.

Dionne's life started far from Los Angeles in Drummondville, Quebec, in 1951. His parents seemed a likely couple to produce a budding hockey star. His dad, an ex-lumberjack who stood 6 feet, 1 inch and weighed 230 pounds, could be expected to pass on some size and power. His mother, meanwhile, had been a fine figure skater. Marcel did take after his mom in skating, starting at the age of two. But he never came close to matching his dad's size.

The Dionnes were a large, close-knit family. Little Marcel was spoiled by his 13 uncles, who often met at the Dionne's old 17-room house. Occasionally, they would pass the hat to raise enough money for Marcel to buy some equipment. Then at games when Marcel would skate around the rink to accept congratulations after a hockey win, he sometimes found some money stuffed in his sleeves. Everyone agreed that the little guy was a tremendous player, but even his family worried that he was too small to go far in the sport.

While growing up, Marcel sought out the best competition that he could find and went to St. Catherine, Ontario, to join a tough junior league at the age of 15. This angered many of his neighbors, who thought he should play for a Quebec team. Teams grew so hot that Marcel's parents faked a separation, and Mrs. Dionne left to live in St. Catherine, which gave Marcel an excuse to stay there to play.

Marcel didn't regret his decision to play in Ontario. There he learned the skills he needed for hockey, as well as the ability to speak English.

He also learned about a player who had stayed back in the Quebec League, Guy Lafleur, and the attention he got overshadowed Dionne. Marcel finally got a chance to play against Lafleur when their teams met for the junior championship in 1971. Unfortunately, some Quebec fans refused to forgive Marcel for being a "traitor." They threw garbage at his family and attacked the Ontario players. Things got so bad that the series was called off with Quebec ahead, three games to two.

Lafleur again edged out Dionne in the 1971 NHL draft. Guy was chosen first by Montreal, and Marcel second by Detroit. The Red Wings' star, Gordie

Young Marcel started quickly as a rookie with the Detroit Red Wings.

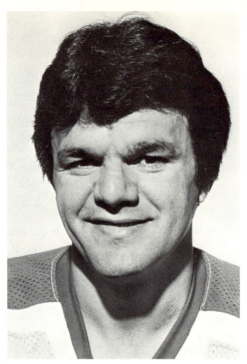

Marcel Dionne

Howe, had just retired, and fans were looking to young Dionne to take his place. The 5-foot, 8-inch center did his best. He outshone Lafleur in his first year and scored 77 points, a league record for rookies. Dionne continued to star for Detroit in the next three seasons. In 1974-75, he reached superstar heights with 47 goals and 74 assists for 121 points. The clever speedster set an NHL record by scoring 10 of those goals while his team was shorthanded due to penalties. At the same time, Marcel was awarded the Lady Byng Trophy for excellence and sportsmanship.

All was not well in Detroit, however. When Dionne saw something he didn't like, he usually spoke up. And he found plenty to talk about with the Red Wings, from the players' carefree attitude to the endless shuffle of new players and coaches. Dionne was called a big baby because of his complaints and was even benched for a couple of games.

When the Los Angeles Kings decided that he was just the sparkplug they needed to get their team going, Dionne could not have been happier. After signing a rich contract, he won over his suspicious teammates and scored 40 goals for the Kings.

As one of the fastest skaters in hockey, Dionne was always a threat to break past the defense for a one-on-one match with the goaltender. He took advantage of his small size to duck under checks and burst out from between two defenders. When that didn't work, he sent defenders sprawling with sharp turns and dazzling footwork. Goalies were constantly on edge trying to figure out his unpredictable tactics. Marcel could keep them guessing about whether he would shoot or pass until it was too late. And although the stocky star constantly spoke out against violence in the game, he was as willing as anyone to take his lumps in the corners.

Dionne's greatest contribution to the Kings' attack was his consistency. Except for the year of

It took awhile for the Los Angeles Kings to adjust to Marcel's style. Here he races in to take the puck from a teammate.

his shoulder injury, 1977-78, Dionne scored 50 or more goals and at least 100 points every season from 1976-77 to 1982-83. Along with teammates Charlie Simmer and Dave Taylor, he formed the "Triple Crown" line (so named because the Kings' uniform emblem is a crown). The group outscored all other lines in the NHL in 1979-80 and 1980-81. Marcel was the man who made the line go, especially in 1979-80. Although both he and Wayne Gretzky totaled 137 points, Dionne won the scoring title for having notched two more goals (53 to Gretzky's 51). The NHL's official Most Valuable Player prize went to Gretzky, but the players chose Dionne for that honor.

Despite all his success, Dionne had taken criticism for his poor showing in Stanley Cup action. Starting in 1978, good Los Angeles teams were blasted out of the play-offs in the opening round for four straight years. During that time, Dionne contributed only one goal and seven assists.

In 1982, though, Dionne gained some satisfaction. In the first round of the play-offs, no one gave

The gold-clad Dionne floats across the opponents' blue line while Butch Goring moves into position to take a pass.

the slumping Kings any chance against Gretzky and the high-scoring divisional champs from Edmonton. But in a wild series of shoot-outs, Los Angeles came out on top. Dionne personally contributed five goals and four assists to the Kings' play-off cause. This, plus his 56-goal showing in 1982-83, proved Dionne to be an exceptional athlete. Even with a team that was finishing dead last in its division, Marcel could still light up the net.

4
Peter Stastny

In August 1980, the Quebec Nordiques secretly joined the international spy world when officials of the NHL club rushed to Europe on a mysterious mission. After a tense series of secret meetings, quiet contacts, and wild car chases through the countryside, the Nordiques narrowly got away with their haul. What could be worth that dangerous battle of wits with secret police from Communist Eastern Europe? A pair of hockey players named Peter and Anton Stastny.

Peter Stastny was born in Bratislava, Czechoslovakia, in 1956. Along with his parents, four brothers, and one sister, he grew up in a one-bedroom apartment. Space was so scarce that most of the children shared beds.

Hockey had become a popular way to pass the winters in that country, and the neighborhood boys sprayed a field outside the Stastny's apartment building to make an ice rink. The three youngest Stastny boys enjoyed the game and followed every bit of hockey news they could find. They talked a lot about Stan Mikita, a Czech who had moved to the United States at an early age. Mikita had teamed with Bobby Hull to give the Chicago Black Hawks the best scoring duo in the NHL in the 1960s.

Local hockey coaches had discovered the Stastnys at play and moved them quickly through the ranks to the Czech national team. Marian, the oldest of the three, led the way as the Czechs stunned the powerful Soviet Union team to win world championships in 1976 and 1977. Their splendid performances made the Stastnys national heroes. They lived up to their roles as ideal models for young boys by accepting their fame modestly and by studying hard at the university.

While the Stastnys were earning applause from their countrymen, great changes were taking place in the NHL. After the U.S.S.R. gave a team of NHL All-Stars all they could handle in a 1972 series, NHL teams began to look at European players with new respect. Before long, the scramble to attract these players to North America was on. More than 50 new stars from Sweden, Finland, and other countries flocked to the NHL in the late 1970s.

Rugged Peter Stastny had no trouble standing up to the rough tactics on the National Hockey League.

Like many pro teams, the Quebec Nordiques dreamed of what it would be like to get the Stastny boys to play for them. But there seemed to be no chance of that happening. Even if the brothers wanted to come to North America to play, their government would not allow it. When the World Hockey Association (of which Quebec was a member) joined the NHL in 1979, the Nordiques started to think seriously about the idea. Desperate to avoid last place in their new league, they plotted several schemes to get the Stastnys. After attempts in West Germany, Italy, and Switzerland failed, the Nordiques looked forward to the 1980 Olympic Games in Lake Placid, New York. With the Stastnys so near, that would be a perfect time to make their move.

But it was not a good Olympics for either the Stastnys or the Nordiques. Although Peter ranked second in scoring in the Games, the Czech team played poorly. They were overwhelmed by the United States, 7-3, and did not even make the final four. Quebec, meanwhile, could not dent the tight security the Czechs had put around their players and were no closer to signing the Stastnys when the Games ended.

Then in August of 1980, the Nordiques received a long-distance telephone call from the Stastnys. The brothers were in Austria for the European championships, and they wanted to talk business. Life had soured for them in Czechoslovakia. In 1979 they had led their local team, Slovan Bratislava,

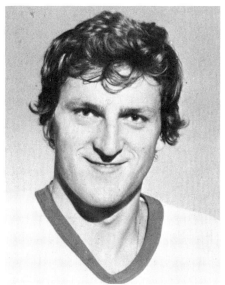

Peter's older brother Marian *(left)* and younger brother Anton *(right)* joined him in providing the Nordiques with instant offense.

to the national title. In a country strongly divided between two groups of people, the Czechs and the Slovaks, the Stastnys were proud to be the first Slovaks to win the country's hockey championship. But the team began to collapse strangely, as if someone wanted to make sure they didn't win again. The coach rarely showed up for practice, and many of the team's best young players were traded to other teams. When the Stastnys complained, they were warned to watch themselves. Despite being heroes, they could be thrown off the national team at the snap of a finger. Fed up with this, the brothers agreed to leave.

Quebec officials rushed to Austria for secret contract talks in a hotel room. They were stunned at how much the brothers knew about the NHL, especially about salaries. The three finally signed, although Marian would have to stay behind. With his wife and children still in Czechoslovakia, he didn't dare leave yet.

After their final game against the Soviet Union, Peter and Anton sneaked out to the dark street where a car was waiting for them. After a nightmarish drive to Vienna, with secret police closing in on them, they boarded a plane for Canada.

Peter and Anton were hardly in a mood to celebrate their escape, however. It was especially hard moving to Quebec where they had to learn not one but two foreign languages, English and French, to get along. They missed their homeland and feared for Marian, who had been dropped from the national team and could not find a job. There was also the problem of adjusting to the NHL's rugged style of play. Many European stars had found that they were not used to the way the game was played in Canada.

Peter, however, scored a goal in his first game as a Nordique. Not even the hardest-checking NHL teams could slow him down. At 6 feet, 1 inch and 200 pounds, he raced down the ice with the speed and grace of smaller men. His long, sharp passes and crisscrossing from side to side with the puck delighted fans and helped his team to score. The only flaw that his coach could find was that he passed too often and did not shoot enough.

With Peter and Anton on the ice, opposing teams could no longer take the Nordiques lightly. Peter

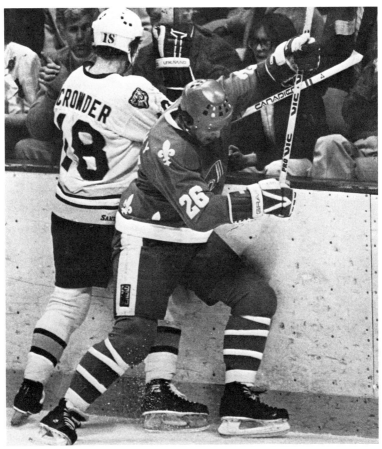

The smooth-skating Stastny shows Boston's Keith Crowder that he's not afraid to battle along the boards.

scored 39 goals and added 70 assists for 109 points that season to win Rookie of the Year honors. That summer there was more good news. Marian had slipped out of Czechoslovakia with his family and would join them for the coming season.

In 1981-82 the three joined forces to make Quebec one of the NHL's highest-scoring teams. With Peter at center, Marian at right wing, and Anton on the left, the Stastnys weaved into the attacking zone with a marvelous show of teamwork. Again it was Peter who did the most to light up

Peter slipped past the Islanders' All-Star defenseman Denis Potvin to challenge goalie Billy Smith in this 1982 play-off action.

the goal lights. He totaled 46 goals and an amazing 93 assists to rank third in the league in scoring. And although Quebec finished fourth in a tough division, they came alive in the play-offs. First, they surprised archrival Montreal, and then they upset the Boston Bruins to gain the Conference finals. There they were stopped by the champion New York Islanders.

Quebec limped through a troubled season in 1982-83. Marian went out with an injury, and several players on the team feuded with the coach. Still, Peter Stastny kept rolling. His 47 goals and 77 assists for 124 points took second place to Wayne Gretzky in the scoring race. With his brothers chipping in 40 goals apiece, the Nordiques had to think that all the money, sweat, time, and worry they had spent getting the three was well worth it.

Even the great Wayne Gretzky could not dent Bryan Trottier's reputation as the best all-around player in hockey.

5
Bryan Trottier

The New York Islanders put together a full roster of stars who led them to three straight Stanley Cup titles in the 1980s. They had Denis Potvin, the NHL's All-Star defenseman; ex-U.S.A. Olympian Ken Morrow; and goalie Billy Smith to shut down opponents. For scoring, they could look to Mike Bossy, Clark Gillies, John Tonelli, Butch Goring, and others. But despite all this talent, the Islanders admitted there was one man they couldn't do without: Bryan Trottier.

Brian was born in 1956 in the prairie town of Val Marie, Saskatchewan. Life was quite simple growing up in the Trottier home: "Do what Dad says to do and don't ask questions." While most young boys in eastern Canada were skating, Bryan was helping out on the family cattle ranch, and he did not learn to skate until he was nine. By that age, many Canadian youngsters had already played hundreds of organized games.

Trottier made up for lost time by cramming his schedule full of games. At age 15, he was playing five games a week. He did well in the junior leagues at Swift Current and Lethbridge, but he did not stand out like Lafleur or Dionne. In 1974 the New York Islanders did not draft him until the second round.

The shy country boy left to join the big city team in 1975 at the age of 19. Although overwhelmed by the different life-style, he did not let it bother his play. Bryan wasted no time in showing the NHL that he meant to make his mark. In the second game of his career, he introduced himself to the Los Angeles Kings by scoring three goals and assisting on two others. Other teams got similar treatment from New York's newest star. Bryan set a new rookie record of 95 points on 32 goals and 63 assists and won Rookie of the Year honors.

The young Islanders improved every season under the guidance of coach Al Arbour. Trottier and All-Star defenseman Denis Potvin gave the club two solid leaders, and Trottier was especially valuable for Arbour's demanding system. The coach insisted on disciplined position play, and a hardworking, high-scoring player like Trottier could set a perfect example for others by carrying out his duties to the letter.

Bryan Trottier

When asked to describe Bryan's greatest talent as a hockey player, most experts would hem and haw for awhile. Most would finally admit that none of his skills really stood out as being tremendous. Trottier didn't rank in the top five NHL players in skating, shooting, passing, stickhandling, checking, or defense. Rather, it was his ability to do *everything* well that made him so valuable.

If opponents wanted to grind it out with a hard-hitting game, Trottier could play that way. Players discovered that, although he stood only 5 feet, 11 inches, Bryan was not a small man. Carrying 195 solid pounds, he hit hard and clean and was tough to knock off his feet. If opponents switched to a fast-skating, wide-open attack, Trottier could handle that, too. Few players as strong as Bryan could pass cleverly and create good scoring chances for teammates the way Trottier could. With a fine sense of position and a good shot, he also scored his share of goals. But best of all, when the game got its most hectic, the Islander star continued to play his cool, fearless game. His skill at winning key face-offs in the closing minutes of tight games helped his team to hang on to many one-goal wins.

In his third year as a pro, Trottier helped rookie Mike Bossy settle into the NHL. He invited the nervous Bossy and his wife to leave their hotel and move in with his family for awhile. The two found they were the same type of guys and agreed to be roommates on the road. Their pace of living was far too slow for most Islanders. Trottier and Bossy spent most of their time during road trips watching TV or talking about hockey, and their idea of going out drinking was to order a couple of milkshakes.

Bossy and Trottier were just as close knit on the ice. One would create the scoring chance, and the other would finish it off. Bryan was so hard to beat in the corners that teams often had to send in two men after him. That left Bossy free to dart

Trottier has Buffalo goalie Don Edwards right where he wants him and sees plenty of open net to shoot at.

in and out in front of the net. When Bryan finally cleared the puck away from the boards, Bossy could slam it in for the goal.

Given Trottier's recent reputation for fine play-off play, it's hard to imagine that he was once accused of crumbling under Stanley Cup pressure. In 1977 the Islanders were knocked out of the play-offs by the underdog Toronto Maple Leafs. Trottier did not contribute a goal in the loss. The following season, he scored 47 goals and 87 assists to capture both the NHL scoring and Most Valuable

Player titles. But in the play-offs, he managed only two goals in 10 games, and the Islanders were again ambushed, this time by their crosstown rival, the New York Rangers. That gave Bryan a grand total of five goals in four seasons of Cup play.

During the 1979-80 season, Bryan came through with a typically fine showing. He played excellent defense, killed off penalty time, centered the Islanders' deadly power play, and led one of the highest-scoring lines in league history. But could he do anything in the play-offs? This time Trottier destroyed all doubts. Setting a play-off record of 29 points on 12 goals and 17 assists, Bryan blazed the way as New York finally captured the famous Cup. He then matched that total the next year, despite playing five games with a separated shoulder. His courageous leadership while injured inspired his team to beat the Minnesota North Stars, 4-1, for the title.

While Wayne Gretzky was wiping out individual records in 1981-82, Trottier did his best to help shatter team records. In midseason, the Islanders set out after the league record of 15 straight wins, a mark held by the Boston Bruins for 42 years. New York breezed through the first 10 games before facing a tough test against the Philadelphia Flyers. Trottier personally took care of the Flyers with five goals to earn victory number 11! When

Trottier shows the Quebec Nordiques that he won't coast on his reputation in 1982 play-off action.

New York broke the old record with their 15th win, they had Bryan to thank. Statistics credited him with six game-winning goals during the streak. The Islanders then breezed to their third and fourth straight Stanley Cups in 1981-82 and 1982-83 without losing a game in the finals.

Despite the incredible records of Gretzky, there were still many who claimed that Trottier was the best *all-around*, all-purpose player in the game. But the guitar-strumming cowboy from Saskatchewan didn't care to get involved in such discussions. Just pass the milkshakes and keep those Stanley Cups coming!

6
Gilbert
Perreault

Critics like to point out that Gil Perreault often skates with the puck too long and has trouble hitting his wings with certain kinds of passes. Although he is large for a hockey forward, he does not use his size well, they say, and he's never been singled out for defensive excellence. On top of that, Perreault has never made a serious bid for a scoring title in his 12 years as a pro. That seems like a grim report on the career of the man who was once considered the NHL's brightest young star. But there is more to the story of the player hockey great Bobby Orr once called "the most exciting player to enter the league in a long time."

Gilbert was born in Victoriaville, Quebec, in 1950. Victoriaville also happened to be the hometown of the Montreal Canadiens' great center, Jean Beliveau. While he was growing up, Gilbert never wanted to be anything but a hockey player, and he tried to copy the style of his hometown hero. Since Perreault was nearly identical to Beliveau in size, temperment, and smooth skating ability, he was a fortunate choice for a model.

Gil went through a Canadian youngster's usual journey to the pros. With plenty of competition at an early age, Perreault had made a name for himself by the age of 11. From there he went on to dominate the Canadian junior leagues under the watchful eyes of NHL scouts. Officials from the two NHL expansion teams were especially interested in Perreault. One of them would have first choice in the draft that year, and there was no doubt that Gilbert was the top player available. The teams sweated out a spin of the roulette wheel to determine which would have first choice. Luck was with the Buffalo Sabres that day, and they eagerly claimed Perreault.

Starting a career in a new country with an inexperienced team was hardly an ideal way to break in. And it was doubly hard for Perreault because he spoke no English. But he picked up the language and caught on to the ways of the NHL just as quickly. The Sabres took care not to put too much pressure on him. They didn't worry about his lack of defensive knowledge; they just wanted him to concentrate on his great offensive talents.

Full speed ahead for Buffalo's star center, Gil Perreault!

Sabre goalie Bob Sauve sits between two-thirds of the French Connection, Rene Robert (left) and Perreault. Sauve seems pleased that he never has to face these two in a game.

Perreault followed his instructions well. Although opposing teams often blasted the Sabres off the ice in 1970-71, Rookie-of-the-Year Perreault fired in 38 goals, an NHL record for first-year players.

During 1971-72, Gil helped to scratch his name from the record books. His puck-handling magic set up newcomer Richard Martin for many shots, and Martin shattered the rookie mark with 44 goals. When young veteran Rene Robert joined the two, Buffalo's famous French Connection was born.

All three players could skate fast, shoot hard, and score often. But the centerpiece of the French

Canadian trio was Perreault. The Sabre center was a master at controlling the puck. Far and away the best stickhandler in the NHL, he could carry the puck through crowds as if it were magnetically attached to his stick. Defensemen found that it wasn't easy to separate him from the puck with a body check, either. At 6 feet and 202 pounds, Gil was strong and had good balance. Not many had a chance to find out how well he could take a hit, though. Perreault had more moves than a disco dancer! With a dip of the shoulder, a couple of head fakes, and a turn of the hip, he could send opponents spinning harmlessly out of the play.

Whereas a camera has to be quick to catch someone like Mike Bossy in the act of scoring, a Perreault scoring highlight often resembles slow motion. No one is better at gathering the puck behind his net, weaving through an entire team with fakes and a burst of speed, and moving in on goal for a shot.

Perreault's French Connection line led the young Sabres as they sped past their more established rivals. During 1972-73, Gil scored 88 points on 28 goals and 60 assists as the Sabres made the play-offs in only their third season. When he sat out for eight weeks of the next season with a leg injury, Buffalo quickly fell out of the play-off picture.

But Perreault's leg healed, and the line came back stronger than ever in 1974-75. The explosive

Sabres put on some incredible shows that year. In February Gil scored two goals and assisted on five others in a 9-5 win. That same year, Buffalo scored eight goals in a single period as they blasted Washington, 14-2. With the French Connection supplying 131 goals, the Sabres swept back into the play-offs.

Still going strong, Perreault and his linemates poured in 18 goals in Stanley Cup action against Chicago and Montreal. With the series against the Canadiens tied at two games each, Buffalo battled Montreal to a tie in game number five. Then Perreault displayed the value of winning a key face-off. Gilbert controlled the dropped puck in the Montreal end and slipped a quick pass to Robert, who fired in the winning goal. The Sabres went on to beat Montreal and move to the finals against the Philadelphia Flyers.

One of the games in the tough championship series was played under nearly impossible conditions. Warm, humid weather combined with the cold ice to form a thick layer of fog over the rink. The game went into overtime, and Perreault again set up the winning shot. Skating through a cloud of fog, Gil dumped a pass to Robert. Robert popped it in before the Flyer goalie could locate the puck. Philadelphia, however, finally took the championship, four games to two.

Perreault's finest scoring year came in 1975-76,

Perreault looks forward to another chance on the ice.

when he collected 44 goals and 69 assists. Teammates Danny Gare and Richard Martin joined him to give the Sabres three men with over 40 goals. But after injuries to Martin, the French Connection line began to fade. Buffalo continued to make the play-offs but no longer challenged for the Stanley Cup, and Perreault was overshadowed by new stars.

The Sabres continued to have moments of brilliance, however. In 1977-78 Buffalo put together a 21-3-3 streak early in the year. Two years later, they advanced to the 1980 Stanley Cup semifinals against the Islanders. Gil slammed in two slap shots

Perreault joins one of his greatest admirers, Boston's Bobby Orr
in a sprint to the puck.

for goals to pull the Sabres to a win in one game.
But the rest of the series went badly, and it was
the Islanders who swept on to the championship.

In his 12th season, 1982-83, Perreault continued
to produce and topped the defensive-minded Sabres
with 79 points. But he no longer won the praise of
those who used to call him the best center in the
game. If Gil had not quite matched the glittering
predictions made for him, perhaps it was because
people were expecting the impossible. For over a
dozen years, the slick Sabres center had treated fans
to some of the most artistic hockey plays ever seen.

7
Dino
Ciccarelli

Minnesota North Stars general manager Lou Nanne watched his fast-skating team control most of the rink during the 1979-80 season. They could move the puck well until it came to those final few feet in front of the goal. Somehow they needed to find another player who could ram that puck into the net. Nanne scoured the lists of professional and junior hockey players and came across the name of Dino Ciccarelli.

The facts showed that Ciccarelli, born in 1960 in Sarnia, Ontario, had moved through the ranks of youth hockey to become an expert goal scorer for the London Knights. In 1978 Dino had even topped the Ontario Hockey League in goals, beating a player named Wayne Gretzky. Although he was a little guy, whose listed measurements of 5 feet, 10 inches and 180 pounds seemed to be stretching the truth, he wasn't afraid of anything. For years Dino had stood up to the most punishing defensive tactics without ever backing down. The little fire-plug had scrapped with just about everyone at one time or other, including a fight with another team's alligator mascot.

Although those facts were known to everyone in pro hockey, not one team bothered to claim Dino when he was eligible for the 1979 hockey draft. That problem could be traced back to a small splinter off a broken hockey stick. Racing down the ice during a hard practice in the spring of 1979, Ciccarelli had tripped on the splinter. He fell heavily and slammed into the side boards. Dino broke his thigh bone so badly that a 16-inch steel rod had to be put into the leg for support. To make matters worse, an infection broke out in the leg.

Since that time, Dino had been working hard with exercises and weights to rebuild the leg, but it was slow going. Ciccarelli tried to skate with the other players, but that was like a raft trying to keep up with a fleet of speed boats. He seldom got to leave the bench during games, and, when he did, it was often for unimportant chores. He was the one chosen to sit in the penalty box when a penalty was called on the London coach. The scouts noticed all this and passed on the word that Dino had no future. As a result, no one drafted him.

That pesky Ciccarelli is on the loose again, leaving Boston's All-Star defenseman Brad Park a stride behind.

Dino uses his time on the bench searching for clues to beating the goalie.

The North Stars, however, wanted to check one more time to see if there was any chance that Dino might return to his old form. When the scouts told Lou Nanne there was no chance of the kid ever making it in the NHL, he checked with Ciccarelli's doctors and heard a different story. They told Nanne that Dino's leg could become completely normal. The North Stars decided to take the doctor's advice, and they signed Ciccarelli.

By the spring of 1981, Ciccarelli had shown he was the best bargain in the entire league. After being called up to the North Stars from a minor league team in Oklahoma City, Dino quickly made a name for himself. Along with his 18 goals in 32 games, Dino drew attention for his showy style of play. Ciccarelli was like a frisky puppy let loose on the ice. He drew raves for scoring while crashing into the net or sliding across the ice on his stomach. Minnesota fans marveled at the way he could draw penalties by taking frightening belly flops when checked by an opponent. And when he scored a goal, Dino could hardly contain his joy.

It's not hard to tell who has just scored a goal for the North Stars!

Unfortunately for Dino, his dancing and flying around on the ice made him almost as many enemies as it did fans. Opponents couldn't quite put their fingers on it, but for some reason the little right winger drove them crazy. He began to feel a lot of hard hits, and he got into all kinds of battles. None of this seemed to affect his play, however, and even the pressure of Stanley Cup play did not disturb the rookie. In a 7-4 semifinal win, Dino got the three-goal hat trick against the Calgary Flames. His extra spark helped push the North Stars into the finals

Islanders Billy Smith and Denis Potvin want to know where Ciccarelli came from to score this play-off goal. In his first play-off season, Dino was practically unstoppable.

against the New York Islanders, where they lost in five games. By the time the play-offs were over, Dino had made a mark that was expected to last for years. His 14 play-off goals were 6 more than the previous record for rookies held by teammate Steve Christoff.

Ciccarelli also had scored more goals in that first full season, 1981-82, than either Wayne Gretzky or Mike Bossy had done in theirs! Breaking the old North Star record of 48 goals held by Bill Goldsworthy, Dino collected 55 and added 57 assists.

In describing his success, most experts used the term jack-in-the-box. Dino simply had a way of popping up at the right place at the right time. Although not one of the fastest on the team in an end-to-end race on the rink, he had quick reactions that helped him spot and reach loose pucks before others did. Like Bossy, Dino got most of his goals on quick flurries. Ciccarelli rarely skated with the puck for very long, preferring to leave stickhandling to others. A typical Ciccarelli goal came on a North Star rush when he was a little behind the action. The puck would bounce off bodies or skates in front of the net, and Dino would beat everyone to it. With a quick flick of his blade, he would pocket the puck in an upper corner of the net. There were those who swore that Dino's goal scoring was mostly a matter of luck. But after leading the North Stars

Ciccarelli's quickness has left many defensemen with their tongues hanging out!

in goals again in 1982-83, Dino showed that there had to be more to it than that.

Ciccarelli is not one of those nervous types who broods for hours before a game. He claims that five minutes is all the time he needs to get himself in the right mood to play. Once the game starts, his concentration is total. It is not unusual to see him staring at the opposing goalie between his shifts, even when the puck is at the other end of the rink. He likes to zero in on the goalie to try and detect any possible weaknesses.

Then, when it's his turn to play, Dino leaps over the board and seems to hop down the ice with his short stride. As his hundreds of young fans wave their plastic "Dino dinosaurs," Ciccarelli seems to be having the time of his life. After nearly missing out on a pro career, Dino Ciccarelli is determined to make the most of his second chance.

Edmonton's Wayne Gretzky: the man everyone comes to see.

8
Wayne Gretzky

Should you envy Wayne Gretzky's Edmonton Oilers teammates, or should you pity them? On one hand, they enjoy the thrill of playing with the man who, by the age of 21, had turned the NHL record book into a scrap pile. Gretzky has fattened their scoring averages by setting them up for easy goals. But on the other hand, it must be discouraging knowing that no one in the arena is paying any attention to you. When Wayne takes his shift, everyone from former pro stars to casual fans can't help but follow *him* around the ice.

Wayne was born in 1961 in Brantford, Ontario, a small city just west of Buffalo, New York. Every winter, his dad would mow the backyard to a stubble and spend nine days forming an ice rink. At the age of two, Wayne was skating on what he later called, "the best ice in Canada." His dad made up special drills such as stickhandling with tennis balls to help his son learn the basics of hockey.

Wayne was an eager student, and he would play hockey with friends after school and then again after supper. If there was a hockey game on TV at night, Wayne would go out and skate between periods. Gretzky caught on to the sport so quickly that he was always matched with boys far older. The only time he was overmatched was as a 6-year-old playing in an 11-year-olds' league. He managed only one goal that year. But as an 11-year-old playing for the Brantford Nadrofsky Steelers, Wayne made a name for himself with 378 goals during the year! At 14 he went to play in Toronto, and by 16 he had moved up to the top Canadian junior hockey league.

Many wondered how the thin Gretzky would survive in the tough NHL. But one advantage of playing with older boys all his life was learning how to avoid hard checks. After signing with Indianapolis (who immediately moved to Edmonton) of the World Hockey Association, Wayne showed he could do more than just survive. Although he was the youngest player in a major pro sport, 17-year-old Wayne scored 110 points to win Rookie of the Year honors in 1978-79.

Edmonton was allowed to join the NHL the next season, and that gave Wayne a chance to match his skills against the best. He started slowly but finished with a furious burst to tie Marcel Dionne for the league lead in points with 137. Nineteen-year-old Wayne became the youngest player to win the NHL's Most Valuable Player Award.

Any remaining critics of Gretzky dashed for cover in 1980-81. The Oilers found that it didn't matter who was on the ice with him; Gretzky could always set up good scoring chances. All of the wingers on the team were given chances to skate with the game's top playmaker. One of Wayne's favorite tricks was to run the offense from behind the opponents' net. With his skill at controlling the puck and threading passes, he had goaltenders spinning. After awhile, opposing defensemen began to go behind the net and wait for him to show up. When that happened, Gretzky adjusted quickly to direct the show from in front of the net. That season he notched an NHL record of 109 assists. His 55 goals gave him 164 points, which easily earned him the scoring crown.

Gretzky's achievements seemed almost impossible when you stood him next to hockey's past stars. Hockey's greatest players have all been powerful men. Rocket Richard, Gordie Howe, Bobby Orr, and Bobby Hull all could overwhelm opponents with their muscle. Nothing short of a bulldozer could move big Phil Esposito from his spot in front

Wayne manuevers around New York Islander defenseman Ken Morrow...

of the net. But Gretzky stood a very thin 5 feet, 11 inches and 170 pounds. He looked sort of frail, and the looks weren't misleading. When the Oilers tested their players for body strength, Wayne came in dead last. He even joked that his shot couldn't break a pane of glass.

Gretzky's success came from the fact that he could make the puck do just about whatever he wanted. Like a control pitcher in baseball who works the corners of the plate, Gretzky usually shot for, and hit, the tiny targets of the upper corners. Also considered the smartest shooter in the

74

NHL, he confused goalies by changing speeds on his shots. Unlike the hair-trigger shots of Mike Bossy, Gretzky often won battles with defenders because of his patience. He could hover near the net with the puck so long that defenders and goalies felt they had to make a move to stop him. Once they did, Gretzky waltzed around them for a score.

When it came to passing the puck, the thin Edmonton center had no equal. Although he often played with unfamiliar linemates, he seemed to be able to calculate where they were going and what

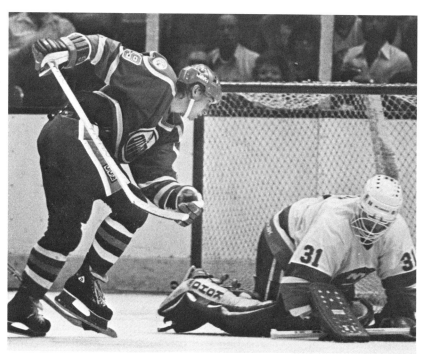

...and challenges Islander goalie Billy Smith.

75

kind of pass was needed to give them the puck. Oiler players have learned to watch out for passes under the most impossible conditions. Once Wayne had the puck behind an opponent's net with defensemen closing in. Seeing a teammate skating alone in front of the goalie, Wayne lifted a pass *over* the net! The result was another goal for Edmonton.

Incidents like that have convinced players that Wayne knew more about hockey than anyone else. His constant study of the game helped him to think ahead on the ice. Most players rushed straight toward the net after a shot, hoping for a rebound. Wayne quickly noted the angle of the shot and skated to where the rebound should bounce, usually to the side. When a puck was passed behind him, Wayne resisted the urge to reach back for it. Instead he kept going and collected the puck when it bounced back to him off the boards.

At the start of the 1981-82 season, most experts declared Gretzky to be the league's best player. But few were prepared for what the Great Gretzky had in store for them. As Wayne and his mates fired in goals at a record pace, opposing goalies suddenly felt as if the net they were protecting had doubled in size. After two months of play, it was already clear that Wayne would make all NHL season scoring records look silly. The famous mark of 50 goals in 50 games by Richard and Bossy was buried under

Gretzky's many duties as a center include taking face-offs, as he attempts to do against Flyer Darryl Sittler in this overhead view.

the Oilers' charge. Gretzky earned *his* 50th in game 39!

Edmonton's simple strategy was to keep Gretzky in the game as long as possible. While most forwards took one-minute shifts on the ice, Wayne often stayed on for three minutes. He killed penalties, directed the power play, and averaged an amazing 38 minutes per game.

It's hard to know where to start to sort through all of Gretzky's records for 1981-82. The "hat trick" (3 goals in one game) is supposed to be one of

Oiler defenseman Al Hamilton is the latest to find out how much fun it is to play hockey on Wayne Gretzky's team.

hockey's most difficult achievements, but Gretzky came up with 10 in one year. In a December game against the Flyers, he scored 5 goals. At one point, he collected points in 30 straight games. In all, Gretzky scored 92 goals that year, 16 more than Phil Esposito's old record. His mark of 120 assists beat his old record of 109, and his 212 points shattered his own scoring record by 48!

Even those astounding numbers cannot fully describe Gretzky's value. The skinny kid who played to exhaustion almost every night still managed 40 of his goals in the key third periods. He assisted or scored on over half of Edmonton's record-breaking 417 goals. As if that weren't enough, he proved to be a deadly marksman. It had taken Boston's Esposito 550 shots on goal to set the previous record of 76 goals. Gretzky earned his 92 goals on just 369 shots!

Wayne's great season could not be overlooked, and nearly all sports publications honored him as athlete of the year. Edmonton's star was mobbed by fans, business executives, and public service groups. He tried to satisfy as many of the demands as he could and undertook a grueling schedule of benefits, public appearances, and endorsements. Somehow, he handled all the publicity quietly and politely and accepted it as part of his job, explaining how his hero, Gordie Howe, had once made his day by signing an autograph for him. Many former stars wondered how long he could keep up with the demands on his time. Some claimed that the reason Gretzky looked so relaxed on the ice was because it was the only time he got any peace!

During 1982-83, Wayne cut back on his personal

appearances but kept up his performance on the ice. He set a new record of 125 assists and led the Oilers to another divisional title and another record for goals in a season: 424. After finishing 70 points ahead of Peter Stastny in the scoring race, Wayne started strongly in the play-offs. His three goals and four assists against Calgary set a scoring record for a play-off contest. And even in his disappointing showing in the finals against the unbeatable New York Islanders, he still managed four assists to give him a play-off record of 38 points.

Despite all his achievements at so young an age, Gretzky hasn't sparked any jealousy among the older stars. Such greats as Bobby Orr, Phil Esposito, and Bobby Hull freely admit that they love to watch Wayne play whenever they get a chance. They also appreciate the lift he has given the game of hockey. Wayne has provided the sport with a refreshing star and has proven that hockey doesn't need ugly brawls to attract fans.

With all he has done, it's hard to remember that the Great Gretzky is still in his early 20s. No one can even guess what the NHL record book will look like once he finishes with it!